DEATH & BISCUITS

JONATHAN YUKICH

BATTEN PUBLISHING COMPANY

Copyright © 2013 Jonathan Yukich

ISBN: 0615808905
ISBN-13: 978-0615808901

Performance Rights

To obtain production and licensing rights, please visit Batten Publishing at battenpublishing.com or email info@battenpublishing.com.

Other Plays by Jonathan Yukich

The Alien From Cincinnati

Alice@Wonderland

American Midget

Balls

Boiling People in My Coffee

The Day the Bird Flu Came

Finding Don Quixote

Frankenstein Unplugged

Thank You, Twenty Thousand Pound Man

CHARACTERS

DOUG

BILL

GRIMM

PATSY

ABBY

SCOOTS

CHAZ

VIVIEN

GASH MANLEY

YOUNG GRIMM

BURT THE BISCUIT

PLACE & TIME

The place is Birmingham, Alabama. The time is 1959.

NOTES ON CASTING

*** The play should be performed with *EIGHT* actors (four men, four women).

*** DOUG and BILL should be played by women.

*** PATSY and GASH MANLEY should be played by the same actor.

*** GRIMM and YOUNG GRIMM should be played by the same actor.

*** More than one actor will need to don the mascot costume to play BURT THE BISCUIT, so this costume should fit multiple performers.

*** Very minor characters, the PA ANNOUNCER and the VILLAGERS, can be easily doubled with members of the cast.

ACT ONE

SCENE ONE

(AT RISE: Through a thin, gloomy mist, CHAZ emerges. He wears a minor league baseball uniform, à la 1959, with the nickname "Biscuits" spelled across the jersey. Spooked and jittery, he holds his baseball bat cocked and ready to strike as he timidly creeps about, searching but wary. As he does, with a thick Southern drawl, he recites the "Lord's Prayer.")

CHAZ: Our Father . . . who art in heaven . . . hallowed be thy name . . . thy Kingdom come . . . thy will be done . . . on earth . . . as it is in heaven . . . Give us this day . . . our daily bread . . . and forgive us our trespasses . . . as we forgive those who trespass against us . . . Lead us not into temptation . . . but deliver us from evil . . . For thine is the Kingdom . . . and the power . . . and the glory . . . for ever and ever –

(In an instant, CHAZ is standing before a coffin, nearly bumping into it. Halting, stupefied, he puts his hand to his mouth, muffling a yelp. Collecting himself, he delicately slides the lid open, peers inside – here lies the evil that lurks! Thinking quick, or as quickly as CHAZ is capable, he breaks the bat over his knee, forming a jagged wooden stake. Tossing aside the shards, he raises the stake above his head.)

CHAZ: AMEN!!!

(As he brings the stake down, we blackout into an organ's "Da-da-da-DA da-DAA!")

SCENE TWO

DOUG & BILL: *CHARGE!!!*

(DOUG and BILL are in the stands to watch their beloved baseball team, the Birmingham Biscuits. Suitably attired in the fashion of the 1950s South, they converse with rapid-fire, red-blooded banter. Both men are played by women — boisterous and blustery, yes, but not parody.)

DOUG: Opening day!

BILL: A fresh start for all!

DOUG: Winter's gone at last!

BILL: And the spoils of spring are nigh!

DOUG: Songbirds and juicy peaches!

BILL: Lush lawns and Mornin' Glories!

DOUG: And baseball!

BILL: America's game!

DOUG: Come to save us!

("Da-da-da-DA da-DAA!")

DOUG & BILL: *CHARGE!!!*

DOUG: Gosh, it's fine to see you, Bill.

BILL: Ditto that, Dougy-doo.

DOUG: How's Bea?

BILL: Well, gee-golly —

DOUG: Trouble at home?

BILL: We're no longer speaking.

DOUG: Why's that?

BILL: We thought it best – to save the marriage.

DOUG: Sometimes it's the only way.

BILL: We still shake hands before bed.

DOUG: Loveless but civil.

BILL: It gets us through. And Edith?

DOUG: Sleeping around.

BILL: What! No! With who?

DOUG: The family vet.

BILL: How do you know?

DOUG: She's covered in cat hair.

BILL: But you have a dog —

DOUG: Bingo.

BILL: How old is Bingo now?

DOUG: Thirteen.

BILL: Maybe it's Bingo's hair.

DOUG: 'Fraid not. Cat dander makes me puffy, and lately I been swelled up like the Michelin Man.

BILL: So it's cat then?

DOUG: Positively. It's as if I'm allergic to my own home, my own wife!

BILL: It don't get much worse than that.

DOUG: She often smells of horse.

BILL: How you holdin' up?

DOUG: Let's just say it's swell to be back at the ballpark. *(Jovially, slapping BILL on the back.)* Same seats as ever.

BILL: *(Returning the back slap.)* Eleven years runnin'.

DOUG: We do love our Birmingham Biscuits!

BILL: More than our wives, I do believe!

DOUG: I'll second that!

DOUG & BILL: Haw! Haw!

> *(BURT THE BISCUIT, a mascot with a biscuit head emerges, revving up the crowd.)*

BILL: Look! It's Burt the Biscuit!

DOUG: Heckuva mascot, that Burt!

BILL: He's lost weight, I think!

DOUG: He's one fit biscuit!

> *(BURT THE BISCUIT pumps his fists, does a jig, cheers, clears.)*

BILL: A lot of excitement this year.

DOUG: Everyone's out to beat the Biscuits.

BILL: Hands down, best team in the Dixie League.

DOUG: We got the bats to take us all the way!

BILL: And the arms to match'em!

DOUG: Word is Adolph Grimm the Fourth has his sights set on taking this team to the Major Leagues.

BILL: That's been his aim since he bought the Biscuits.

DOUG: This could be the year.

BILL: If all goes well.

DOUG: How can it not? With our talent!

BILL: Look there! It's Adolph Grimm in his box seats!

DOUG: Why so it is! Our beloved owner . . .

(ADOLPH GRIMM THE FOURTH appears, wearing his customary all- white suit and cooling himself with a hand fan.)

GRIMM: *(Breezily requesting a "corn dog.")* Would some dear soul be so charitable as to fetch me a *cone dawg*?

PATSY: *(Presenting a corn dog, with servile promptness.)* As you say, sir.

GRIMM: Bless you, Patsy.

(Lights out on GRIMM and PATSY.)

BILL: Imagine that wouldja! The first Major League baseball team from the South: the Birmingham Biscuits!

DOUG: Has a ring, don't it!

BILL: We're already the first in the South to have night games!

DOUG: Let there be lights, spaketh Mr. Grimm! And it came to pass!

BILL: The Giants to Cisco, the Dodgers to L.A.! It's 1959 and the Big League's spreadin' out quicker than commies in D.C.! They're just beggin' to come South!

DOUG: They say Atlanta's posturing to be the first.

BILL: Fat chance.

DOUG: They're spending millions on an *"international"* airport over there.

BILL: Lotta good that's gonna do'em!

DOUG & BILL: Haw! Haw!

DOUG: If it's anybody, it'll be us.

BILL: That's the straight dope.

DOUG: And Mr. Grimm's got the money to make it happen!

BILL: Where's that daughter of his?

DOUG: Oh, Abigail Joe?

BILL: Over yonder! In the bleachers!

DOUG: It's Abigail Joe alright.

> *(Lights up on ABIGAIL JOE, or ABBY. She wears a hitting helmet, on backwards, and a baseball glove, which she chews.)*

BILL: All by her lonesome.

DOUG: She don't know no difference.

BILL: How long's it been since the accident?

DOUG: Several years now.

BILL: Foul ball to the head.

ABBY: *(With cross-eyed daffiness.)* I like Biscuits!

DOUG: Bless her heart.

BILL: Ain't been the same since.

DOUG: Gone wacky but still loves baseball!

BILL: Must be the smells!

> *(Lights out on ABBY.)*

DOUG: Ah, the smells! Sodypop and crackerjacks!

BILL: Pine tar and cigarettes!

DOUG: Old leather and roasted peanuts!

BILL: Fresh dirt and man sweat!

DOUG: What a game!

BILL: Say it twice!

DOUG: What a game! What a game!

BILL: Howdy-doo!

("Da-da-da-DA da-DAA!")

DOUG & BILL: *CHARGE!*

DOUG: Say, Bill, take a peep at the new pup – first base line.

BILL: Must be that Scoots McGhee kid.

DOUG: Grapevine says he's awful fast.

BILL: He looks scared to death.

(Lights up on SCOOTS, in a Biscuits uniform, stretching his legs, talking to himself. A trickle of blood runs from his nose.)

SCOOTS: Keep it together, Scoots. It's the Dixie League, for Pete's sake, not the Majors. You're as good as anyone out here.

(CHAZ TROUTLY, the ultra-confident, all-everything athlete, appears taking some practice swings.)

CHAZ: What's the matter with you?

SCOOTS: What? Nothing.

CHAZ: Your schnoz – it's runnin' like a hose.

SCOOTS: Oh no – again!

CHAZ: Did you overstretch?

SCOOTS: Sometimes when I get nervous my nose bleeds.

CHAZ: That never happens to me.

SCOOTS: Nose bleeds?

CHAZ: Getting nervous. Name's Chaz Troutly, reigning Dixie League MVP.

SCOOTS: Chaz Troutly! You're the hottest prospect in America!

CHAZ: Is that what they say?

SCOOTS: Sure is. You're going to be a Major League star!

CHAZ: Keep it together, nosebleed. Where you from?

SCOOTS: Just off the bus from Bismarck.

CHAZ: Georgia?

SCOOTS: North Dakota.

CHAZ: That's a state?

SCOOTS: It's relatively new.

CHAZ: Well plug your muzzle, huh, before you stain your uni. And straighten your cap! I got scouts here to see me!

(CHAZ walks off.)

SCOOTS: Sure thing, Chaz.

(Lights out on SCOOTS.)

DOUG: That Chaz, he's sure a winner.

BILL: The best we'll ever see.

DOUG: I sometimes dream of Chaz.

BILL: Him playing ball?

DOUG: Just doing chores around the house, like dishes or laundry. The other night I dreamt he was mowing my lawn. I took him fresh lemonade and said something amusing. We chuckled and sipped.

BILL: That's kinda peculiar, Doug.

PA ANNOUNCER: Ladies and gentlemen, please rise with hands over hearts, to honor our nation. Performing tonight's National Anthem is Birmingham's own organ sensation, 97 year-old Cookie Putnam.

(Lights up on all – BILL, DOUG, GRIMM, ABBY, SCOOTS and CHAZ – rising and standing at attention, each in their own way.)

DOUG: Cookie's back for another year.

BILL: I reckon she'll croak at that organ.

(Cookie and her squeaky organ are heard playing the National Anthem. After a few bars, VIVIEN enters,

hand over heart. She possesses a stern, distinguished flair about her. To the disbelief of everyone present, she is dressed as the home plate umpire.)

CHAZ: What the – ?

GRIMM: *(Dropping his corn dog.)* Jiminy Christmas.

BILL: Doug, am I deceived, or is that –

DOUG: Unthinkable.

SCOOTS: Holy heckfire.

ABBY: *(Suddenly lucid.)* What have we here?

DOUG: In all my years –

CHAZ: You're dreaming, Chaz.

SCOOTS: A lady umpire –

BILL: I feel like I'm seeing Bigfoot.

CHAZ: *(Willing it so.)* Just a dream, just a dream.

DOUG: It's an abomination.

CHAZ: Any moment monkeys will fall from the sky and play banjos.

GRIMM: Patsy? Where'd you go?

ABBY: Something's afoot.

GRIMM: Patsy! We've got a situation!

ABBY: Definitely afoot.

BILL: She'd have to squat. Ladies can't squat – on dirt, in public!

DOUG: What if she menstruates in the middle of a rally!

BILL: There are children present!

DOUG: She'll bleed all over the diamond!

BILL: And attract bears, to boot!

CHAZ: *(Looking to the heavens, panicky.)* Where are the monkeys? There must be monkeys!

GRIMM: Who let that home plate whore into my ballpark!

CHAZ: Oh Lord, it's really happening.

SCOOTS: I declare.

GRIMM: Patsy!

ABBY: Let the game begin.

(The National Anthem ends.)

VIVIEN: PLAY BALL!!!

(Lights out on all but Vivien.)

SCENE THREE

(VIVIEN pulls down her umpire's mask. GASH MANLEY, chewing a big wad of tobacco, is at the plate. VIVIEN speaks with a very faint Eastern European accent.)

VIVIEN: STRIKE THREE!!!

GASH: Bull malarkey!

VIVIEN: You're out!

GASH: The ball was low!

VIVIEN: *(Removing mask.)* It was down the middle.

GASH: You're off it!

VIVIEN: Take a seat.

GASH: Don't boss me!

VIVIEN: I made my call.

GASH: Is this a ballgame or a circus!

VIVIEN: It *used* to be a ballgame.

GASH: You think you're big stuff, don't ya?

VIVIEN: You struck out – you sit down.

GASH: The hell I will!

VIVIEN: Then I'll toss you out of the game.

GASH: As if you could!

VIVIEN: I'm the umpire.

GASH: You ain't got the brass!

VIVIEN: So be it! You're outta here!

GASH: You gonna make me?

VIVIEN: You push me too far.

GASH: Chased by a dame!

VIVIEN: I'm warning you.

GASH: You already tossed me – what else you gonna do?

VIVIEN: I have methods.

GASH: I ain't takin' orders from no woman blue. You'll have to drag me from this field kickin' and screamin'.

VIVIEN: That can be arranged.

GASH: What a gas! You're just a – you know what you are? You know what word I'm thinkin'?

VIVIEN: I do not.

GASH: *(In her face; steely, callous.)* I think you do. I think you know the word I'm thinkin'. I'm thinkin' it right now, and so's everybody else in this ballpark. You know the word. You know what you are.

(GASH exits, staring down VIVIEN all the way off.)

(BURT THE BISCUIT enters to whimsical organ music, and begins a belittling dance directed at VIVIEN. This includes giving her the thumbs down, making bunny-ears behind her, fanning his rear at her, kicking dirt on her, and other crude denigrations. This eggs on the crowd. As BURT'S dance of ridicule intensifies, we hear escalating boos and jeers. VIVIEN, with seething restraint, can only stand and endure.)

SCENE FOUR

(MR. GRIMM in his office with a frazzled, irate CHAZ.)

CHAZ: I'm ruined!

GRIMM: It wasn't your best game.

CHAZ: Four strikeouts!

GRIMM: Everyone has bad days.

CHAZ: I'm not everyone! I'm Chaz Troutly!

GRIMM: Still the finest centerfielder in the game.

CHAZ: I'm washed up!

GRIMM: Dear boy, it's but one game.

CHAZ: There's no future for me outside baseball!

GRIMM: Don't vex yourself, champ.

CHAZ: Doctor, lawyer, president – I ain't got the training, Chief!

GRIMM: This is true.

CHAZ: I'm an 8th grade dropout! It's the Big Leagues or bust!

GRIMM: And that's where you shall land – in due time.

CHAZ: No, now! I gotta make the Bigs now, Chief!

GRIMM: Why the rush?

CHAZ: I need that Big League dough.

GRIMM: You in trouble, Chaz?

CHAZ: Naw.

GRIMM: You been bettin' the cockfights again?

CHAZ: It ain't that. I'm just – I'm ready for my shot, I guess – and she's gonna ruin it!

GRIMM: It's being handled, my boy. As we speak, Patsy's escorting the person of interest to my office.

CHAZ: You gonna throw her in jail?

GRIMM: We're gonna chat – equably.

CHAZ: And then you'll throw her in jail.

GRIMM: And then she'll come to her senses.

CHAZ: And *then* you'll throw her in jail.

GRIMM: I won't be throwing her in jail, Chaz.

CHAZ: She's dirtied our past time!

GRIMM: Chaz, Chaz, Chaz – in 24 hours, this will have all blown over. You have my word. So forget it ever happened, and come to the ballpark tomorrow night and play like the Chaz Troutly we all adore.

CHAZ: They'll still adore me?

GRIMM: You're a treasure, Chaz. Say, I should have you over to the house for supper soon. I'll serve chicken marsala – and we'll all three have a grand time.

CHAZ: Can we just pretend tonight never happened?

GRIMM: It's the beautiful thing about baseball: there's always a game tomorrow to help you forget today.

CHAZ: You say there'll be *three* for dinner?

GRIMM: Oh, yes, Abigail Joe.

CHAZ: Ain't she tarnished?

GRIMM: She has her tics.

CHAZ: I really drilled her with that foul ball a few years back.

GRIMM: I think it would be good for the two of you to start spending more time together. You're like a son to me, Chaz, and Abby's like a, well —

CHAZ: A daughter?

GRIMM: No — oh, yes, of course! You know, she's made real progress since you nearly killed her. You two may hit it off.

CHAZ: I like chicken.

GRIMM: Then it's a date! *(Putting his arm around CHAZ.)* Meantime, relax: take a bath, rub yourself down, and leave this mess to me.

CHAZ: Say, what's that on your neck?

GRIMM: What's what?

CHAZ: That spot.

GRIMM: Oh that. A birthmark is all.

CHAZ: I never noticed.

GRIMM: Every Grimm has an identical mark in the same place. Obstinate are the ways of progeny. Now you get on now.

CHAZ: You'll clean this up?

GRIMM: Have I ever not?

CHAZ: I'm counting on you.

(CHAZ exits as PATSY enters.)

GRIMM: Well? Where is she?

PATSY: I don't know if she's coming.

GRIMM: Not coming?

PATSY: There's something queer about her.

GRIMM: Did you give her my note?

PATSY: I don't recall.

GRIMM: But you were just there.

PATSY: Yes.

GRIMM: So did you give it to her or not?

PATSY: I was on my way to deliver the note when I heard commotion coming from Burt the Biscuit's locker room. Then I see *her* exit the locker room.

GRIMM: What would she want with Burt?

PATSY: Got me.

GRIMM: She saw you?

PATSY: With eyes like black rivers. I peered into them, and the next I know I'm walking back into your office. She's queer, sir, and dare I say, wondrous.

GRIMM: She made an impression, I see.

PATSY: She's real plush alright. But I must've given her the note. It ain't on my person.

GRIMM: Then she's making us wait.

PATSY: What's with Chaz?

GRIMM: He thinks we're doomed.

PATSY: It's not so bad as that.

GRIMM: We were ghastly tonight.

PATSY: We'll turn the corner.

GRIMM: This was supposed to be the year of the Biscuit.

PATSY: It may yet be.

GRIMM: Not with her calling games.

PATSY: I thought she umpired a good game.

GRIMM: She's in the players' heads – you can see it. A woman in baseball! And of all things, an umpire! I'm just glad Daddy Grimm didn't live to see this – it might've killed him.

PATSY: Give a woman a bit of power –

GRIMM: And she'll plunder your soul.

PATSY: You're upset. I'll make you a Shirley Temple.

GRIMM: It's no use.

PATSY: No? How about a maraschino cherry?

GRIMM: Gimme the jar.

(Taking the jar, GRIMM begins to pop cherries into his mouth.)

PATSY: Why not just fire her?

GRIMM: I don't have the authority. Umpires are hired by the league.

PATSY: Seems odd we weren't notified of this lit-fuse in advance.

GRIMM: Does indeed. *(Slight pause.)* May I confide in you, Patsy?

PATSY: By all means.

GRIMM: This rumor about me wanting to take the Biscuits to the Majors?

PATSY: All of Birmingham is talking.

GRIMM: It's more than rumor.

PATSY: *(Gasp.)* Well shut my mouth.

GRIMM: The Major League's looking to add another team. I was to put in a bid at the end of this year. Figured we'd stand as good a chance as any. Of course, all this was predicated on the Biscuits winning the Dixie League, and Chaz blooming into a major star.

PATSY: Which is in reach.

GRIMM: Was, Patsy, *was.* All that's blowin' by a thread now. The Major League's got no interest in a losing Southern ballclub whose best player is a meatheaded man-child. All we'll be known for is that team that had the first woman umpire. We'll be the laughingstock of baseball!

PATSY: But as the saying goes, "The only bad publicity is –"

GRIMM: Horse shit.

PATSY: Right.

GRIMM: Birmingham needs this. We were hightailing down the road to glory, but the fates have placed a speed bump before us. And what, I ask, does a great man do when confronted with a speed bump? What would Napoleon or

Herbert Hoover have done? What would Daddy Grimm have done?

PATSY: Go around?

GRIMM: He wipes it out!

PATSY: Yes, that's better.

GRIMM: He obliterates whatever stands in his way!

PATSY: I'm getting goose chills.

GRIMM: Pleasantly we'll ask for her resignation; with luck, she'll accept and we can put this whole affair to bed. But if she refuses, if she plays the proverbial hardball, then I'm afraid we have only one option left to us: Code Blue.

PATSY: Code Blue?

(VIVIEN has entered.)

VIVIEN: You have asked to see me?

(At her voice, PATSY squeaks in fright.)

GRIMM: *(Hospitably.)* Ah, at last! Come in, come in! Patsy, get the lady a chair! *(PATSY hustles to do all he's told.)* I'm so grateful you've come. The night is late.

VIVIEN: For some.

GRIMM: Can I get you something? Do you drink?

VIVIEN: Oh yes.

GRIMM: Perhaps a hot toddy?

VIVIEN: Nothing now, thank you.

GRIMM: You are very pretty out of uniform. Black becomes you.

VIVIEN: Cease your curtsies, Mr. Grimm. Why am I here?

GRIMM: That's precisely what I want to ask you.

VIVIEN: To determine ball from strike.

GRIMM: To be an umpire.

VIVIEN: A lifelong dream.

GRIMM: Listen, Miss – um?

VIVIEN: Vivien Stahl Von Dieterhoff.

GRIMM: *(Distracted.)* I feel as though I recognize you from somewhere.

VIVIEN: Yes?

GRIMM: Though I'm sure we haven't met.

VIVIEN: I have this effect on people.

GRIMM: Your accent –

VIVIEN: I am from a small village in the south of Austria.

GRIMM: Is that so? You know, my bloodline is Austrian.

VIVIEN: Delicious.

GRIMM: Pardon?

VIVIEN: Delightful.

GRIMM: Patsy, sit down and quit hovering. You're making me nervous.

PATSY: Right. Yes sir. *(Sitting.)* Hi, Miss – Miss Vivien. Remember me?

VIVIEN: Of course. You are the messenger.

PATSY: My name is Sylvester, but everyone calls me Patsy.

VIVIEN: I've gathered.

GRIMM: How does a girl from southern Austria come to be an umpire?

VIVIEN: When my family came to America, I fell in love with the game.

GRIMM: Then you must know that it's a man's game, and that your presence has proved unsettling.

VIVIEN: My judgment is as acute as any man's.

GRIMM: You're mistaken. A woman's brain is half the size. Read the science.

VIVIEN: What science?

GRIMM: It's out there.

VIVIEN: Show me.

GRIMM: Viv, the ballpark is where men go to escape. It's all we have. Your being here threatens that, ergo it threatens the greatest game ever invented. And we can't have that.

VIVIEN: You are driving at?

GRIMM: I'm asking you to desist – to resign.

VIVIEN: I see.

GRIMM: You'll save us all a season of grief. What d'ya say? Let's all go back to how things should be, huh.

VIVIEN: This is what you wanted?

GRIMM: Yes.

VIVIEN: Goodbye then.

GRIMM: So you'll resign?

VIVIEN: My being here, Mr. Grimm, means more than you know. I will not quit.

GRIMM: I can make it worth your trouble.

VIVIEN: Are you trying to bribe a league official?

GRIMM: I'm a man of consequence, Ms. Dieterhoff. I'm the Paper Clip King of the South. I've grown the family business into an empire, and built this team – my pride and joy – with my bare hands.

PATSY: And all that with a name like Adolph.

GRIMM: The name isn't what it used to be.

VIVIEN: Are you quite through?

GRIMM: It's going to take more than an uppity umpire with lipstick to take me down.

VIVIEN: We shall see. The Biscuits have 55 home games this season and, I assure you, for each you shall see me behind home plate. And, for the record, I do not wear lipstick.

GRIMM: I regret it has to be this way.

VIVIEN: It's always been this way.

GRIMM: *(Again detecting a resemblance.)* Are you sure we haven't met before?

VIVIEN: You cannot place me?

GRIMM: No, no I can't. Perhaps a previous life, huh?

VIVIEN: Perhaps you are more right than you know.

(VIVIEN exits.)

PATSY: *(Taken with Vivien's flair.)* Wow! She is really something!

GRIMM: Patsy, I have a task for you.

PATSY: More cherries?

GRIMM: Murder.

PATSY: What!

GRIMM: Code Blue. If we're to save this team, she must be eliminated.

PATSY: Oh, I just couldn't –

GRIMM: You don't love the Biscuits?

PATSY: Well sure I do, but I'm a Baptist!

GRIMM: Naturally, you'll want it to look like an accident: a bus wreck, or snake bite –

PATSY: No way!

GRIMM: Try to keep it orderly.

PATSY: I won't!

GRIMM: And if you could have it done by tomorrow night's game –

PATSY: Are you listening? I refuse!

GRIMM: Patsy, you dare disobey me?

PATSY: I could never take a human life. You'll have to do it yourself!

GRIMM: Out of the question. I can't have blood on my hands – or, worse yet, on my suit.

PATSY: Then you'll have to find some other.

GRIMM: Hm. I reckon I will. *(Switching tactics.)* I only hope whoever I find . . . won't mind becoming General Manager.

PATSY: General Manager? Of the Biscuits?

GRIMM: Why, yes, did I not mention that? Whoever does the hit, gets the job.

PATSY: I've wanted that title for years.

GRIMM: Which is why I thought you'd be grateful for the opportunity.

PATSY: But to take a life –

GRIMM: Think of your city.

PATSY: It's too much to ask.

GRIMM: Think of your team.

PATSY: I'd hate myself.

GRIMM: Think of your dream job.

PATSY: I'll kill her.

GRIMM: We may get to the Majors after all.

SCENE FIVE

(ABBY, surrounded by cryptic books, diagrams, and charts. Chomping an apple, she reads intently, about to arrive at some obscure, intellectual revelation.)

ABBY: Just as I thought! The electromagnetism of the sun reverses the metabolic process, thus reducing the dead flesh to vapors! It makes perfect sense!

(SCOOTS comes crashing in, lost and flummoxed.)

SCOOTS: I'm, uh, I didn't mean to –

ABBY: Who are you!

SCOOTS: I'm real sorry.

ABBY: *(Brandishing a stake.)* Identify yourself or I'll rip open your heart!

SCOOTS: I'm Scoots! Scoots McGhee – I'm a Biscuit!

ABBY: *(Advancing.)* Spawn of Satan!

SCOOTS: I'm only a second baseman!

ABBY: Who sent you! Who!

SCOOTS: No one! I thought this was the way to the parking lot!

ABBY: Damnation!

SCOOTS: Please! It's my first day at the ballpark!

ABBY: Get thee to hell, demon! *(About to strike, hesitates.)* What's with your nose?

SCOOTS: It bleeds when I'm excited.

ABBY: Why would you be excited?

SCOOTS: Rip open heart?

ABBY: You're a Biscuit, you say?

SCOOTS: I played in tonight's game!

ABBY: Second base? Three errors – you were awful.

SCOOTS: Opening day jitters.

ABBY: Then you're not one of them?

SCOOTS: One of who?

ABBY: You couldn't be, of course. I didn't invite you in. Their kind has to be invited in. I nearly staked you for no reason. I should be more careful. Here's a Kleenex.

SCOOTS: I'm just gonna go –

ABBY: Wait. How about some green tea?

SCOOTS: It's been a long day.

ABBY: I apologize for trying to impale you. Being cooped up like this, I get nervy.

SCOOTS: *(Still rattled.)* I'm over it already.

ABBY: We've gotten off on the wrong foot.

SCOOTS: It's nothing. This kind of thing happens all the time.

ABBY: That's true.

SCOOTS: It is?

ABBY: I always think the worst of people, and regret it later.

SCOOTS: Wait a second, I saw you in the stands. You were sucking your glove.

ABBY: Yes, that was me.

SCOOTS: I thought you were –

ABBY: What?

SCOOTS: Afflicted.

ABBY: I live dual lives, Mr. McGee.

SCOOTS: So all that was put-on?

ABBY: By day, I'm the slow-witted owner's daughter, by night I'm –

SCOOTS: You're Mr. Grimm's daughter!

ABBY: Call me Abby. My life's work requires a degree of subterfuge.

SCOOTS: What's your life's work?

ABBY: Please, take a Kleenex – you're making me sick.

SCOOTS: *(Takes a Kleenex.)* Thanks.

ABBY: You won't tell anyone that you've seen me like this?

SCOOTS: Like what?

ABBY: *Unafflicted.*

SCOOTS: Oh, I wouldn't, no. But why do you pretend so?

ABBY: Born a comely girl, I was just a bit of property to daddy, a handsome trophy to sweeten some lunkhead's contract. He balked at my intellectual pursuits, dismissed them as pataphysic nonsense. I was destined to be the wife of a ball player, some pee brain with a .230 lifetime average. Then I got hit by Chaz's foul ball, and the idea came to me: no stud's gonna pick a filly who limps. Ever since I've feigned "damaged goods." No one bothers me, and I've never been more productive.

SCOOTS: Must get lonely, though, being hushed away in here. What is this place?

ABBY: It's the inside of the left field scoreboard. Used to, someone would sit in here and update the score manually. This one's been abandoned since daddy put the electronic one in center.

SCOOTS: You sit in here –

ABBY: In secret. You're the first to find me.

SCOOTS: It's your office?

ABBY: And home. I live in here. Got a pillow, a lamp, a hot plate –

SCOOTS: *(Picking one up.)* And all these books –

ABBY: *(Quickly snatching the book from him.)* Hey hey, nosey pants!

SCOOTS: What is it you do in here?

ABBY: I'm a protector, of sorts.

SCOOTS: A protector from what?

ABBY: You'd only scoff.

SCOOTS: Promise I won't.

ABBY: From dark forces.

SCOOTS: Socialists.

ABBY: Vampires.

SCOOTS: In Jesus name!

ABBY: I'm a vampire hunter.

SCOOTS: You really think they –

ABBY: After today, I've never been so certain.

SCOOTS: They're among us?

ABBY: In this very ballpark.

SCOOTS: I need another Kleenex.

ABBY: My family has a tangled history with vampires – as this book proves. *(Hands Scoots a small, aged book.)* The diary of my great-grandfather: Adolph Grimm the First.

SCOOTS: What's in here?

ABBY: You really want the history?

SCOOTS: I think I do, sure.

ABBY: Well, you see, my great-grandfather, being an avid diarist –

> *(YOUNG GRIMM appears, wearing lederhosen, now a bright-eyed teenage boy, recording in his diary.)*

YOUNG GRIMM: Dear Diary: Ah, how the open air of the Austrian mountainside does a young boy good!

SCOOTS: I don't read German.

ABBY: I'll translate. The early entries are typical of a teenage boy.

YOUNG GRIMM: Dear Diary: Skating season is fast approaching! My relay squad has a chance to be best in the *Bundesland*! How pleased this would make papa!

ABBY: But the tone gradually shifts –

YOUNG GRIMM: Dear Diary: I fear strange happenings loom ahead . . .

ABBY: Turning ominous –

YOUNG GRIMM: Of late, two mates from my relay squad have vanished, quite inexplicably. It is highly out of character for Johann and Siegfried to miss practice. Their disappearance adds to the growing number of local young boys mysteriously gone missing. The villagers detect a plague, of the most deadly sort!

ABBY: They should have been so lucky!

(VIVIEN appears, a foreboding countess of the night; somewhat younger, fresher.)

VIVIEN: Hello, young man.

YOUNG GRIMM: Hello ma'am. I trust I'm not on your land.

VIVIEN: No no, you're just where I'd like you.

YOUNG GRIMM: It's so pleasing to sit beneath the moonlight and chronicle my thoughts.

VIVIEN: May I join you?

YOUNG GRIMM: Your company is most welcome.

VIVIEN: *(Moves beside him.) Danke.*

YOUNG GRIMM: I love this spot most. See how the moonlight spills into the valley like liquid silver.

VIVIEN: Magnificent.

YOUNG GRIMM: And the stars! Aren't the stars splendid?

VIVIEN: *(Eyes fixed on the boy.)* A revelation.

YOUNG GRIMM: So many. No matter how many you account for, more seem to pop up.

VIVIEN: Just like young boys.

YOUNG GRIMM: Yes, sort of. How do you mean?

VIVIEN: *(Backpedaling a bit.)* Cycle of life. We're young, we grow old, and there are always children to fill the void, repeat the cycle. As plentiful as stars, they are, the children of the night.

YOUNG GRIMM: Oh, I like that very much! Stars are as children of the night! It's evocative!

VIVIEN: I dabble in the poetic arts.

YOUNG GRIMM: Such an august night, don't you think! I could just die and go to heaven!

VIVIEN: Mmmm . . .

SCENE SIX

(GASH in a bar, The Double Play, spouting off drunk. He holds a beer bottle.)

GASH: And then she has the gall to strike me out! A woman! Strikes me out! Me! Gash Manley! I hit seven triples last year! And this is what I get! It's disgraceful is what it is! A national goddamn travesty! Gimme another beer!

(VIVIEN appears, alluringly.)

VIVIEN: Hello, Gash.

GASH: Speak of the she-devil.

VIVIEN: I've been searching for you.

GASH: You have?

VIVIEN: Buy you a beer?

GASH: Man buys the woman beer.

VIVIEN: Buy me a beer?

GASH: Hell no. What do you want with me?

VIVIEN: I came to smooth things over.

GASH: Hope you brought a steamroller.

VIVIEN: Truth is, I may have been a little rash earlier tonight.

GASH: Goddamn right.

VIVIEN: I regret what happened between us – the words exchanged.

GASH: You were out of line.

VIVIEN: I was, yes.

GASH: You got no business on that field.

VIVIEN: I'm coming around to that view.

GASH: The ball was low.

VIVIEN: Possibly a shade low.

GASH: Basically in the dirt.

VIVIEN: You're probably right. I'm just a woman trying to save face. May I join you?

GASH: I reckon.

VIVIEN: You're quite strapping, Gash.

GASH: This is something I know.

VIVIEN: I have a weakness for headstrong men who speak their mind.

GASH: That's natural.

VIVIEN: I think under different circumstances we might have hit it off.

GASH: Well, maybe the circumstances are changing.

VIVIEN: I might like that.

GASH: Yeah? You got a name?

VIVIEN: Vivien. Call me Viv.

GASH: Viv, huh?

VIVIEN: It's Latin for "Life."

GASH: Gash is American – for "cut open."

VIVIEN: At the risk of being too forward –

GASH: You wanna get outta here?

VIVIEN: How's my place?

GASH: Okie-doke.

VIVIEN: Fabulous. *(Waves her hand.)* Why don't I put on some music?

GASH: Whoah!

VIVIEN: Something wrong?

GASH: How'd you do that?

VIVIEN: Do what?

GASH: It was like you waved your hand and we were back at your place.

VIVIEN: But that would defy natural law, Gash. You've had too much to drink. *(Waves hand again. Music is heard.)* Do you like the Drifters?

GASH: I think I need to sit down.

VIVIEN: Nonsense. Let's dance.

(They sway to the music.)

GASH: I've never been with an umpire before.

VIVIEN: Progress brings opportunity. Come closer.

GASH: I can't resist your smell. What is that?

VIVIEN: Talcum.

GASH: I'm gonna kiss you now.

VIVIEN: Yes . . .

GASH: Are you ready?

VIVIEN: I think so.

(He kisses her, breaks away.)

GASH: Ah, you're a biter.

VIVIEN: Oh dear, what have I done?

GASH: I'm okay. It's just a nick.

VIVIEN: I'm afraid I haven't much practice.

GASH: You shouldn't use your teeth.

VIVIEN: Intimacy makes me twitchy.

GASH: Let's try again. This time, relax and let me do the work.

(They kiss again, this time smoothly. It turns into heavy petting. VIVIEN begins to smooch his neck.)

GASH: That's the stuff.

VIVIEN: This is right?

GASH: Oh yes.

VIVIEN: You like my nibbling?

GASH: Uh-huh . . . you're real keen at this part.

VIVIEN: I'm a neck gal.

GASH: I'll say. Feels good.

VIVIEN: Gash?

GASH: Don't stop.

VIVIEN: Gash?

GASH: Yeah, shug?

VIVIEN: I lied earlier.

GASH: All's forgiven.

VIVIEN: It was a strike.

GASH: Excuse me?

VIVIEN: It was down the middle, you hick piece of trash!

(With great and sudden ferocity, Vivien lets loose a snarling hiss.)

GASH: Jesus Christ! *(She locks her fangs into Gash's neck.)* Ah, ah, teeth again – Viv? Goddang, woman! Help! Help!

(Vivien breaks his neck, then finishes sucking his blood. She lets the corpse drop to the floor, wipes her bloody mouth with the back of her hand.)

VIVIEN: Cunt.

SCENE SIX

(Resuming with SCOOTS and ABBY.)

SCOOTS: You're saying this was the woman your great-grandfather bumped into?

ABBY: I have no doubt.

SCOOTS: It's pretty nutballs.

ABBY: If you're gonna demur, you can just adios.

SCOOTS: I'm not *demur-er-er-in*. It's just, if the stranger was a vampire wouldn't she have sucked his blood there on the mountainside?

ABBY: I wasn't finished.

SCOOTS: There's more?

ABBY: Much. It's true, that night her aim was to feast on my great-grandfather – but something extraordinary happened.

(YOUNG GRIMM and VIVIEN at a moonlit mountainside.)

VIVIEN: Ever waltzed in the moonlight, young man?

YOUNG GRIMM: I've never even waltzed in the daylight.

VIVIEN: Would you care to?

YOUNG GRIMM: Waltz? With a woman?

VIVIEN: There's no one else.

YOUNG GRIMM: We haven't any music.

> *(Vivien waves her hand, the music of Johann Strauss is heard in the distance.)*

VIVIEN: But haven't we?

YOUNG GRIMM: Herr Strauss!

VIVIEN: Must be coming from the village.

YOUNG GRIMM: He's superb!

VIVIEN: Rise and take my hand.

YOUNG GRIMM: I'm not sure I know how.

VIVIEN: I'll lead.

> *(They come together.)*

YOUNG GRIMM: I'm so pleased I've had someone to share this night with.

VIVIEN: Me too.

YOUNG GRIMM: Can we be friends?

VIVIEN: For as long as you live.

YOUNG GRIMM: You're very polite.

VIVIEN: *(Sizing up her bite.)* I try. Can you angle your head?

YOUNG GRIMM: Like this?

VIVIEN: Tilt a bit more.

YOUNG GRIMM: Better?

VIVIEN: Perfect.

YOUNG GRIMM: You're very pretty too.

VIVIEN: Yes.

YOUNG GRIMM: And cultured.

VIVIEN: *Oui oui.*

YOUNG GRIMM: And you have the most incredible smile lines.

VIVIEN: *(Taken with the remark.)* What did you say?

YOUNG GRIMM: When you smile, the lines around your eyes – they're very warm and lovely.

VIVIEN: My smile lines.

YOUNG GRIMM: They're exquisite.

VIVIEN: I've never been told such.

YOUNG GRIMM: It's silly of me, I know, but it's the first thing I note when a person smiles.

VIVIEN: Oh?

YOUNG GRIMM: Have you smiled much, ma'am?

VIVIEN: There was a time.

YOUNG GRIMM: You really should, you know. Your face is mapped for happiness.

VIVIEN: *(Moved.)* In all my centuries, those are the kindest words ever spoken to me.

ABBY: And from that point on she was smitten.

SCOOTS: All over a little compliment.

ABBY: The heart's a riddle, even for the undead.

YOUNG GRIMM: Centuries?

VIVIEN: I mean years, of course – though my time on this earth has been long. At last, however, I see a light – before me.

ABBY: Each night hence, they would meet at the same spot.

SCOOTS: Romantically?

ABBY: They'd sit on the mountainside, under the moonlight, holding hands and taking in the night.

YOUNG GRIMM: Vivien, your hand's like ice.

VIVIEN: I'm cold by nature.

YOUNG GRIMM: Perhaps some gloves would help.

VIVIEN: Your warmth is all I require.

YOUNG GRIMM: You speak too highly of me. I'm a mere schoolboy.

VIVIEN: Every hell has a heaven, and you are mine.

YOUNG GRIMM: Once, before we met, I mistakenly fell asleep on this very spot. I awoke to a most glorious sunrise.

VIVIEN: I've imagined many sunrises.

YOUNG GRIMM: You've never seen a sunrise?

VIVIEN: Oh, thousands – who hasn't? But, still, describe the one you saw, won't you?

YOUNG GRIMM: Like rousing to a waiting paradise. As if a gift had been bestowed on me from above.

VIVIEN: You sound almost holy.

YOUNG GRIMM: A sunrise converts quicker than scripture. But my gaiety did not last. Father found me and blistered me with the switch.

VIVIEN: He must have been worried.

YOUNG GRIMM: I disappoint him, I'm afraid. I was hoping to win the championship speed-skate meet. This would bring him pride. Local winners are invited to Vienna for nationals! Alas, though, we placed second. I've failed him yet again.

VIVIEN: You are hard on yourself.

YOUNG GRIMM: He's right about me. A stargazer is all I'll ever be.

VIVIEN: I don't like these sentiments.

YOUNG GRIMM: At least I have you, and our nights together.

VIVIEN: Perhaps you will still go to Vienna.

YOUNG GRIMM: How do you mean? We lost.

VIVIEN: Accidents happen.

ABBY: And – wouldn't you know! – the first place team suddenly vanishes, forfeiting the championship to Young Grimm's squad. Coincidence?

SCOOTS: Could've been.

ABBY: Baloney.

YOUNG GRIMM: *(Giddy.)* We're going to Vienna!

VIVIEN: What? A miracle!

YOUNG GRIMM: The other squad's come up missing.

VIVIEN: What good fortune!

YOUNG GRIMM: So we're to go in their stead! Oh, till now I've only dreamt of seeing Vienna! Come with me!

VIVIEN: Oh now, that's senseless.

YOUNG GRIMM: You can see me skate!

VIVIEN: But I've already seen you.

YOUNG GRIMM: You have?

VIVIEN: Every meet since we met.

YOUNG GRIMM: But I haven't seen you there.

VIVIEN: I'm there. I'm always there – watching.

YOUNG GRIMM: Please come to Vienna!

VIVIEN: I cannot. Cities are too confining for a country creature like myself. For once in a long while, you'll be free of me.

YOUNG GRIMM: Then I'll bring you back something! What would you like?

VIVIEN: Foolish boy.

YOUNG GRIMM: Vienna has everything you could want!

VIVIEN: I want nothing.

YOUNG GRIMM: Some perfume? How about a nice Viennese fragrance?

VIVIEN: Well, I am nearly out.

YOUNG GRIMM: That's it then! I'll bring back Vienna in a bottle! Oh, I'm so happy!

VIVIEN: *(Genuinely.)* As am I.

ABBY: Here the unraveling begins.

SCOOTS: But they seem swell.

ABBY: It's in Vienna that Adolph Grimm meets his true love.

SCOOTS: Oh no. Who is she?

ABBY: The perfume girl.

VIVIEN: It seems you've been away months!

YOUNG GRIMM: *(Withdrawn.)* Only a few days.

VIVIEN: Is everything okay?

YOUNG GRIMM: I have something to tell you.

VIVIEN: I want to hear all about Vienna, but first – my perfume.

YOUNG GRIMM: What perfume?

VIVIEN: The perfume you said you would – *(Sensing disaster, braces herself.)* What is it you want to tell me?

YOUNG GRIMM: I've met another.

VIVIEN: Another *what*?

YOUNG GRIMM: Woman.

VIVIEN: How pedestrian.

YOUNG GRIMM: We're in love.

VIVIEN: This can't be.

YOUNG GRIMM: I have a bit of money saved. I'm moving to Vienna to be with her. This is our last night together.

VIVIEN: But I gave you all.

YOUNG GRIMM: What we have can't last.

VIVIEN: Why not?

YOUNG GRIMM: I've had some time to reflect, and realized you're kind of creepy.

VIVIEN: Is it because I go on about wolves? You can just tell me to shut up.

YOUNG GRIMM: It's many things, Vivien.

VIVIEN: But my smile lines?

YOUNG GRIMM: They're more just wrinkles.

VIVIEN: *(Hurt.)* I see. Well then, a hug for the road?

YOUNG GRIMM: If you'd like.

VIVIEN: I would, yes, thank you.

> *(They embrace.)*

YOUNG GRIMM: I won't forget you.

VIVIEN: This is the end.

YOUNG GRIMM: I'm afraid it has to be.

VIVIEN: Yes it does.

YOUNG GRIMM: Can we still be friends?

VIVIEN: For as long as you live.

YOUNG GRIMM: I knew you'd take this well. *(Vivien unleashes her ferocious snarl.)* Vivien!

VIVIEN: One way or another, I shall have you!

> *(Vivien locks her teeth into his neck.)*

YOUNG GRIMM: Ahhhh!!!

> *(There is a struggle; Young Grimm manages to break loose.)*

VIVIEN: *(Mouth dripping with blood.)* You can't escape.

YOUNG GRIMM: Monster!

VIVIEN: I suck you because I love you!

YOUNG GRIMM: Beastly wretch!

VIVIEN: These names you use!

YOUNG GRIMM: All of Europe shall know of the devil that hunts the night!

(YOUNG GRIMM scampers off.)

VIVIEN: I may be a vampire, but I'm also a woman! You can run, young Adolph, but I will find you!

ABBY: But before she could, Adolph informed the whole village about the vamp of the fields.

SCOOTS: They assumed he was crazy?

ABBY: They would have, but he had THIS!

(ABBY reveals a bite imprint on her neck.)

SCOOTS: You've been bitten!

ABBY: Not really, don't be afraid. When you survive a vampire bite, the mark stays in your bloodline forever. I'm proof my great-grandfather was bitten.

SCOOTS: Then he must've lived on.

ABBY: After he warned the village, he became a hero. His father was so proud he gave his son his life savings, which he used to start his paper clip company. This is how he made his fortune. The Grimm family owes it all to a vampire.

SCOOTS: What became of Vivien?

ABBY: The villagers chased her deep into the mountains.

(VILLAGERS enter, with clubs and lanterns.)

VILLAGERS: There she is! Get'er! Yar! Rar! Grrr!!!

(They chase VIVIEN off, but she halts for a final word.)

VIVIEN: I'll have my revenge! One day! You'll see! You'll ALL see!!!

ABBY: And there she dwelt, living in caves, surviving on the blood of rodents. It was far too risky to come out. Instead, she plotted her revenge, patiently waiting, like any good vampire, for the right opportunity to pounce. Until tonight, no one had seen her for nearly a century.

SCOOTS: She's the umpire!

ABBY: You're catching on, Scoots.

SCOOTS: Right in front of us!

ABBY: Vampire umpire.

SCOOTS: It even rhymes! Oh, she's bold!

ABBY: I know how the vindictive devil thinks. Rather than simply murder my father, she wants to make him suffer first – by slowly wrecking his greatest love.

SCOOTS: The Birmingham Biscuits.

ABBY: It's not by accident she's come back as an umpire. Loss by loss, she toys with her prey. And she won't rest until she destroys the family name! She has to be stopped.

SCOOTS: I want to help.

ABBY: I could use someone on the inside.

SCOOTS: Where can we get garlic and holy water?

ABBY: You have much to learn.

SCENE SEVEN

(In a dark alley, PATSY spills his bullets. He clambers to pick them up, talking to himself.)

PATSY: Klutz, what are you doing here? "Thou shalt not kill" – no denying the essence of that clause. And lookatcha!

(A figure enters sprinting, gasping. PATSY, alarmed, clumsily puts on a ski mask and hides. The figure is CHAZ. His hair is tussled and his clothes slightly torn. Out of breath and exhausted, he collapses.)

PATSY: *(To himself.)* Chaz . . . ?

(Before PATSY can assist him, a rustling is heard as VIVIEN enters from the opposite direction, dragging a very full, very heavy garbage bag.)

VIVIEN: *(To herself, grousing.)* Disposing of the body: the part you never see in vampire films. *(She sees Chaz's supine body.)* They're certainly making it easy for me here . . .

CHAZ: *(Seeing her, wheezing.)* You again!

VIVIEN: You don't look so hot.

CHAZ: Who asked ya!

VIVIEN: I can help, if you'd like.

CHAZ: Why do you haunt my life?

VIVIEN: You may need medical attention.

CHAZ: I'm fine. Just gotta get to my feet . . .

(She helps him up. Chaz winces at the pain in his hand.)

VIVIEN: Your hand pains you.

CHAZ: It's my non-throwing hand.

VIVIEN: You have a dislocated thumb.

CHAZ: It's just a sprain.

VIVIEN: It'll only get worse if you don't set it.

CHAZ: You a doctor now too?

VIVIEN: I'm versed in many subjects.

CHAZ: You're partly to blame for this, you know.

VIVIEN: I don't see how.

CHAZ: I struck out four times tonight!

VIVIEN: You're dropping your elbow.

CHAZ: You're a real know-it-all, ain't ya? What are you doing in this alley anyway?

VIVIEN: The trash isn't going to take itself out.

CHAZ: It's after midnight.

VIVIEN: I keep a tidy home.

CHAZ: Looks heavy. What is it?

VIVIEN: Old plants.

CHAZ: *(Moving past her.)* Well, I've seen plenty of you for one day.

VIVIEN: *(Peering over his shoulder.)* Say, are you being followed?

CHAZ: Where! *(As Chaz turns his back, Vivien grabs his hand.)* What're you –

VIVIEN: This will hurt.

(She yanks his thumb back into place.)

CHAZ: Yooowwwwwww!!!

VIVIEN: It had to be done.

CHAZ: You crazy bird! That hurt!

VIVIEN: As I said.

CHAZ: Sonuva!

VIVIEN: All better now.

CHAZ: *(Wiggling thumb, surprised.)* Well, yeah, sorta is.

VIVIEN: You're welcome. Who did this to you?

CHAZ: Why do you care?

VIVIEN: *(Turning to go.)* I don't.

CHAZ: Bookies. Cockfight bookies. They run this town.

VIVIEN: You owe money.

CHAZ: Thousands.

VIVIEN: That's where betting cocks will get you.

CHAZ: I ain't even a gambler.

VIVIEN: Seems otherwise.

CHAZ: Just need money quick.

VIVIEN: For what?

CHAZ: Family stuff.

VIVIEN: Say more.

CHAZ: My kid sister, she's one of the gifted sorts, see. No joke – like a genius.

VIVIEN: What's she have to do with cockfights?

CHAZ: I promised that when it came time for college I'd find a way to send her. Told her if she had the grades, I'd have the money, thinking I'd be in the Bigs by now. Well, she's sure got the grades, and I sure ain't got the money, not with no measly minor league salary.

VIVIEN: You have parents?

CHAZ: We was orphaned when I was twelve. I took care of her since. Done the best I could. But now I'm in over my head.

VIVIEN: You've been running for your life.

CHAZ: How can you tell?

VIVIEN: Experience.

CHAZ: I've owed too much for too long. They woulda killed me just now, but I got away. They're prowlin' after me as we speak.

VIVIEN: I can help you.

CHAZ: I don't want no help from you. I hope they boo you off the field tomorrow.

VIVIEN: Why say such things?

CHAZ: You don't belong.

VIVIEN: Would you wish that on your sister?

CHAZ: 'Course not. She's different.

VIVIEN: She's a woman. They'd boo her, same as me, for that fact alone. If she's as bright as you say, she has much grief ahead.

CHAZ: *(Reconsidering.)* You got money?

VIVIEN: No, but I can protect you. From the bookies. Until you get to the Majors.

CHAZ: You?

VIVIEN: Guaranteed.

CHAZ: This is scum of the earth we're talking about, men with guns and moustaches.

VIVIEN: They're no match for me.

CHAZ: You're out to lunch, lady.

PATSY: Lord help me! High glory!

(Masked, PATSY makes his move, leaping into sight, gun pointed. VIVIEN takes the gun and, with uncommon strength, crushes it in her hands. She then grips petrified PATSY by the throat, chokes him unconscious, and tosses him aside.)

CHAZ: *(Impressed.)* When can you start?

VIVIEN: I already have.

CHAZ: Should I come home with you?

VIVIEN: You're safe, trust me.

CHAZ: Somehow, I do.

VIVIEN: I'll never be far.

CHAZ: Let me dump your trash for you.

VIVIEN: No no, I can manage.

CHAZ: It's no problem.

VIVIEN: *(Adamant.)* Please. I like doing these things myself.

CHAZ: Fine, okay. You really are a whatsit – a feminist.

VIVIEN: Guilty.

CHAZ: Why are you nice to me?

VIVIEN: People seldom surprise me.

CHAZ: I surprised you?

VIVIEN: There's more to you than people might think.

CHAZ: That's what sis says. *(Brief pause.)* Your eyes –

VIVIEN: Dark and deep, I know.

CHAZ: Something else . . .

VIVIEN: My mascara? It's Maybelline.

CHAZ: Your smile lines. You have pretty smile lines. That's what it is.

VIVIEN: *(Touched.)* Oh Chaz . . .

CHAZ: I knew there was somethin'.

VIVIEN: It's been so long.

CHAZ: Are you about to cry?

VIVIEN: You darling boy. Perhaps you should come home with me.

CHAZ: It ain't about hanky-panky is it?

VIVIEN: I'll only tend to your wounds.

CHAZ: I could use some tending.

VIVIEN: And, later, if the mood is right, we can go up on the roof.

CHAZ: And count the stars?

VIVIEN: *(Tenderly.)* And count the stars.

(Lights fade.)

END OF ACT ONE

ACT TWO

SCENE EIGHT

(AT RISE: The bloodied corpse of BURT THE BISCUIT. The mascot, splayed and listless in his locker room, has been roundly slaughtered. GRIMM and PATSY look on in quiet disbelief. PATSY'S face is bruised and he wears a neck brace.)

GRIMM: *(With resigned despair.)* This morning I awoke to a nightmare. It featured a woman umpire. So unseemly was my vision that I had the shakes, quite literally, Patsy. My palpitations had returned and a cold sweat enveloped me.

PATSY: But you don't sweat –

GRIMM: It's only a dream, I told myself, *convinced* myself. I was elated at the thought. Revitalized. My most bitter fears dissipated. Scrambled eggs have never tasted so succulent. Chickadees have never sung so prettily. On the drive to the ballpark, I found myself in a state that can only be described as rapturous. However, my jubilation has come to a swift impasse.

PATSY: Who would want to kill a biscuit?

GRIMM: And of all biscuits – Burt?

PATSY: Horrible.

GRIMM: How was it done?

PATSY: Looks like his throat was torn in two.

GRIMM: Biscuits have throats?

PATSY: You realize there's someone inside the costume.

GRIMM: Right right.

PATSY: A college student named Jasper. Became the mascot just so he could get into games for free. That's how much he loved the Biscuits. And now – this. So pointless.

GRIMM: Poor Burt.

PATSY: Jasper.

GRIMM: Him too.

PATSY: I'll call the police.

GRIMM: I don't believe that's necessary.

PATSY: But it's clearly a homicide.

GRIMM: We can't have Burt's death in the headlines.

PATSY: Forgive me, sir, but some things are more important than business and baseball.

GRIMM: Spare me your lectures, Patsy.

PATSY: What other option do we have?

GRIMM: We stash the body and solve this from within.

PATSY: Stash it where?

GRIMM: *(Contemplates.)* The right field bleachers. No one sits out there.

PATSY: But won't people wonder why Burt's so detached?

GRIMM: I see your point. There's nothing more suspicious than a melancholy mascot.

PATSY: And how would we explain the bloodstains?

GRIMM: There's that.

PATSY: Children loved Burt.

GRIMM: We all loved him. Scratch the bleachers! We'll put him inside the left field scoreboard! It's been empty for years!

PATSY: But no one ever goes out there.

GRIMM: That's why it's perfect.

PATSY: But we'll forget about him – then he'll fester and rot and smell up the whole ballpark.

GRIMM: *(Frustrated.)* Then hack him into small pieces, if you have to, and toss him in the river. How hard can it be to dispose of a dead biscuit?

PATSY: *(Leery.)* You want me to hack him up?

GRIMM: Post haste. It has to be done. *(Noticing his bruises and brace.)* What happened to you?

PATSY: Oh, uh, Code Blue.

GRIMM: You finished her?

PATSY: She's the devil.

GRIMM: Come now Patsy.

PATSY: She broke my gun like a candy bar and tossed me through the air like a ragdoll! She ain't regular, sir – no she ain't. And look! *(Beside Burt's corpse, he lifts an umpire's mask.)* Her mask!

GRIMM: How can a lesser sex cause such carnage?

PATSY: Like I say, she's more monster than woman!

GRIMM: *(With cowed acceptance.)* I can deny it no longer. It must be her.

PATSY: Who?

GRIMM: A fiend from the past.

PATSY: I don't follow.

GRIMM: Family lore tells of a vampire who, over a century ago, fell in love with my great-grandfather. He betrayed her and she vowed vengeance. Now, I believe, she's returned.

PATSY: Vampire? In Birmingham?

GRIMM: All signs would indicate. Abigail Joe, at least before her accident, was sure this would happen. She was always asking how I could deny my birthmark.

PATSY: What birthmark?

GRIMM: *(Showing the spot on his neck.)* This here.

PATSY: Holy mother! You've been bitten!

GRIMM: My ancestor was bitten. A trace of her venom stays in the bloodline.

PATSY: Then you're part vampire?

GRIMM: Which could explain my business prowess. In truth, until now, I thought Abby was flaky for believing in all that hokum. Now I realize I should have listened to her. If only she were of sound mind, she'd know what to do.

PATSY: Why doesn't she – or *it* – just finish you off?

GRIMM: She's waited too long to simply take my life. She'll toy with me first – as a cat would a chipmunk. Ruin my fortune, my family, my team. In only a day, she's taken the Biscuits from a Dixie League powerhouse to probable cellar dweller. She's also devoured our mascot. Yet I fear it's only the beginning.

PATSY: Your fortune's too big to take down.

GRIMM: *(Defeatist.)* Paper clips aren't what they used to be.

PATSY: Sure they are.

GRIMM: Don't play me for a fool, Patsy. We both know the common stapler has revolutionized paper fastening. I've been toppled by modernity. All I have left – my future, my legacy – is tied up with this team.

PATSY: Then it's imperative she's stopped.

GRIMM: Her kind is too strong. Soon I too shall buy the farm, just as our friend Burt here.

PATSY: This hem-and-hawing isn't like you.

GRIMM: What's the use anymore?

PATSY: *(Uncharacteristically assertive.)* You're acting like you just had your lunch money stolen!

GRIMM: Know your place, Patsy.

PATSY: Where's the man whose guff I've blindly followed for most of my adult life!

GRIMM: He's still here.

PATSY: The man who stuffs his pillowcase with fresh dollar bills at night!

GRIMM: I've always slept better on cash.

PATSY: Who once golfed with the Vice President and accused him of cheating!

GRIMM: Nixon shaves strokes – ask anyone.

PATSY: Who once called the New Deal a commie takeover!

GRIMM: *(Rallying.)* It's true.

PATSY: The sort of man who stays and fights to a certain death, rather than run away like any sensible person with a shred of forethought!

GRIMM: That sounds like me.

PATSY: You've built this team from red dirt and fool's luck! And now you're just gonna let it slip away!

GRIMM: By God, you're right, Patsy. We've got to fight this.

PATSY: Dang right we gotta! Fight it and win!

GRIMM: This is a side of you I haven't seen before.

PATSY: *(Unsure of himself.)* Baffling, isn't it?

GRIMM: I don't know where I'd be without you. You know, you're more than a faceless underling to me – you're also a loyal subordinate.

PATSY: *(Proud.)* Thank you, sir.

GRIMM: Our only hope is to get to Vivien before she gets to us.

PATSY: There's plenty of ways to kill a vampire.

GRIMM: Don't be too sure. Abby used to say you'd be naïve to go by books or movies. No, according to Abby, there's only one way to be sure of destroying a vampire and that's –

SCENE NINE

(ABBY with SCOOTS, on a hillside watching the sunrise.)

ABBY: – to locate its tomb and stake it through the heart.

SCOOTS: While she sleeps?

ABBY: If you're smart about it.

SCOOTS: But how do you sniff out a vampire's tomb?

ABBY: With great cunning. For centuries the vampire has survived by excelling at the simplest of nursery school games: hide-and-seek.

SCOOTS: Has one ever been caught?

ABBY: Oh sure. The Biter of Beijing was staked, beheaded and burned in 1804. Then there was the Succubus of the Yucatán – staked, beheaded, burned in 1870. And, who can forget the De Lucas? A family of vampires in turn-of-the-century Chicago. Eventually they were –

SCOOTS: Staked, beheaded, burned?

ABBY: And buried in cement. Ties to the Mafia.

SCOOTS: You sure know your vampires.

ABBY: I'd better. I'm seeking to codify their history, science and mythology into a 20-volume opus. The work would serve as a unifying key to understanding the vampire's place in our physical world. It may take a lifetime, but I'm determined to finish it. Nothing like it has come before, and nothing will after. There aren't many things you can say that about.

SCOOTS: I love you.

ABBY: I'm sorry?

SCOOTS: You're the top.

ABBY: Scoots –

SCOOTS: I love you.

ABBY: No you don't.

SCOOTS: I do.

ABBY: Don't.

SCOOTS: Do.

ABBY: Why're you telling me this?

SCOOTS: Ma always said: when you find *the one*, don't stop telling her.

ABBY: So she was psycho too?

SCOOTS: It feels good to have it off my chest.

ABBY: We've barely met.

SCOOTS: We've spent a night together.

ABBY: I don't think so.

SCOOTS: I do. See – the sun's rising.

ABBY: Dawn?

SCOOTS: They say a Southern sunrise bides its time.

ABBY: I've talked all night.

SCOOTS: You can talk all morning too, if you like.

ABBY: You must be so sick of hearing about vampires.

SCOOTS: Not a bit. I love –

ABBY: Quit saying that. Are you thick?

SCOOTS: You're pretty, and smart, and spirited –

ABBY: And very wedded to my work.

SCOOTS: There's no room for romance?

ABBY: How can you bring this up at a time like this?

SCOOTS: Like what?

ABBY: There's a vampire in our midst.

SCOOTS: Right, almost forgot. So what do we do? How do we find her tomb?

ABBY: Reconnaissance. Wait and watch.

SCOOTS: Spy on her?

ABBY: The best we can. Vampires sense when they're being followed. They can slink into shadows, contort into strange critters.   It can take weeks, even months to pin one down.

SCOOTS: I'll do all I can.

ABBY: We can't rest until we've erased this black-hearted wretch from the earth.

SCOOTS: Will you go out with me tonight after the game?

ABBY: What did I just say?

SCOOTS: One milkshake.

ABBY: I shouldn't really –

SCOOTS: You can tell me more about the 12th century vampires of Malta.

ABBY: I barely touched on that tonight.

SCOOTS: It's part of my tutelage.

ABBY: The Maltese are an interesting lot.

SCOOTS: So yes?

ABBY: One milkshake, then we hunt evil.

SCENE TEN

(DOUG and BILL in their seats at the ballpark. They look miserable and downtrodden. "Da-da-da-DA da-DAA!" rings out.)

DOUG & BILL: *(Barely audible.)* Charge . . .

BILL: It was supposed to be our year.

DOUG: I believed.

BILL: We all believed.

DOUG: Six won, fourteen lost.

BILL: It's like they've caught a disease that's made them forget how to play baseball.

DOUG: Just three weeks ago we were oozing confidence.

BILL: That was before the Medusa –

DOUG: The Helen –

BILL: The Pandora unfurled her wrath.

DOUG: *(Leaping to his feet and shouting at the field.)* GO MAKE A CASSEROLE, TOOTS!

BILL: Nice one.

DOUG: *(Sitting again; glumly.)* Even belligerent slurs have stopped being fun.

BILL: The ballpark used to be my church.

DOUG: Nothing's the same.

BILL: Except for Chaz.

DOUG: The only bright spot.

BILL: He's playing lights out.

DOUG: He's a force of nature.

(Pause.)

BILL: A few months back Bea suggested a love suicide.

DOUG: A what?

BILL: Love suicide. When all love is gone from a relationship, the couple, rather than stew in their unhappiness, takes their lives together.

DOUG: People do such things? In the suburbs?

BILL: More than you'd think. It's kind of a courtly hara-kiri, but with cyanide and Pepsi.

DOUG: That's crazy talk.

BILL: That's what I tell her – or used to tell her.

DOUG: Things aren't much rosier on my end.

BILL: Edith still seeing the veterinarian?

DOUG: The other day I took Bingo in for his shots. Routine visit. The nurse calls us back, and I mistakenly open the door to the wrong room. And there's Edie, on the exam table naked – with Dr. Brightly squatting over her, wearing only an X-Ray jacket.

BILL: My Jesus.

DOUG: He was having her from behind.

BILL: Appropriate, given the location.

DOUG: *(Choking up.)* Thing is, I look at myself and I don't blame her, not in the least.

BILL: Hey now – you're a good man.

DOUG: Am I? Then why do I got this hole inside me?

BILL: It's just a rough patch is all.

DOUG: It's so hard.

BILL: It'll pass.

DOUG: I just needed something good to happen.

(DOUG breaks into tears. Consoling, BILL places his hand on DOUG'S knee.)

BILL: Hey hey, buck up, Dougy.

(Without thinking, DOUG puts his hand on top of BILL'S. There is a wide silence. Both men look at one another, confused. BILL then places his other hand on top of DOUG'S. Another bewildered look. DOUG places his remaining hand on top of BILL'S. At last, DOUG and BILL gently kiss. The kiss is sweet, and lasts a brief moment, before they hastily break away.)

DOUG: You know what the Biscuits really need is a bullpen.

BILL: I've said that for years.

DOUG: The bullpen's always been our Achilles.

BILL: You'd think we'd learn.

DOUG: Pitching wins baseball.

BILL: Yes it does.

DOUG: Yes it does.

BILL: Yes . . . it . . . does . . . *(Strained pause.)* Well, this one's out of hand. I'm gonna get going.

DOUG: It's the fifth inning.

BILL: We're down six runs.

DOUG: But we never leave early.

BILL: I had a long day at the office.

DOUG: At least stay till the Stretch.

BILL: I'm gonna get going.

DOUG: I'll see you tomorrow then?

BILL: I'll beat the traffic this way.

DOUG: See you tomorrow, Bill?

BILL: It's better like this.

DOUG: Bill?

BILL: *(As if saying goodbye forever.)* You take care of yourself, Dougy.

> *(BILL leaves. DOUG sits alone, unsettled and frightened by nearly everything.)*

SCENE ELEVEN

> *(Between innings, VIVIEN stands filling in her scorecard. CHAZ is a few paces away, taking practice swings in the on-deck circle. They speak surreptitiously, never making eye contact.)*

VIVIEN: The southpaw's off his game.

CHAZ: I didn't ask.

VIVIEN: He's leaving his curveball up.

CHAZ: Hush it.

VIVIEN: Likes working the outer half.

CHAZ: You shouldn't tell me these things.

VIVIEN: I thought you'd want to know, since you're standing there.

CHAZ: I'm on-deck.

VIVIEN: My tips aren't useful?

CHAZ: It's cheating.

VIVIEN: I only do it for you.

CHAZ: You gotta stop.

VIVIEN: Whatever you say.

CHAZ: You know I was doing pretty good on my own.

VIVIEN: I said I'd stop.

CHAZ: Good.

VIVIEN: Expect a first-pitch fastball.

CHAZ: Viv.

VIVIEN: That's the last of it.

CHAZ: You're supposed to be impartial.

VIVIEN: See you after the game?

CHAZ: Can't tonight. Mr. Grimm's having me over for late supper.

VIVIEN: Grimm, huh? I thought we were going to the picture show.

CHAZ: You've seen the flick five times.

VIVIEN: It's a classic.

CHAZ: It's not my speed.

VIVIEN: How do you know? You fall asleep.

CHAZ: Thankfully.

VIVIEN: Murnau's *Sunrise* is one of the great achievements of your time.

CHAZ: *Our* time.

VIVIEN: I have no time that belongs to me.

CHAZ: What's that supposed to mean?

VIVIEN: Sorry, I can't help being dramatic.

CHAZ: You have a real flair for that.

VIVIEN: We'll meet up after your dinner?

CHAZ: Your place. I'll come there as soon as I can.

VIVIEN: It'd be a shame to waste such a clear night.

CHAZ: Viv, can I ask you somethin'?

VIVIEN: Whatever you like.

CHAZ: Where do you go off to in the mornings?

VIVIEN: Mornings? Oh – breakfast.

CHAZ: Why don't you wake me?

VIVIEN: You need your rest.

CHAZ: I sleep with you at night, but you're never there in the morning. In fact, I don't see you at all till I get to the ballpark the next day. I'm tempted to fake like I'm sleeping just to follow you.

VIVIEN: You must never.

CHAZ: What if I did? What if I were to follow you?

VIVIEN: *(Turning her eyes on him; sharply.)* Chaz, you must never.

CHAZ: Touchy.

VIVIEN: Do you understand?

CHAZ: Sure, yeah. Sorry I asked.

VIVIEN: Batter up!

> *(VIVIEN dons her umpire's mask and moves off. SCOOTS appears, also taking practice swings.)*

CHAZ: Hey, nosebleed, you got a girl?

SCOOTS: Kinda, yeah.

CHAZ: You like her?

SCOOTS: Oh, she's super swell.

CHAZ: I got one too.

SCOOTS: I bet they line up for you – you're Chaz Troutly.

CHAZ: This one's different than the others.

SCOOTS: Mine's special too.

CHAZ: Yeah?

SCOOTS: I'm falling for her – *hard*.

CHAZ: Yeah? How do you let on?

SCOOTS: Let on?

CHAZ: Show that you really like her.

SCOOTS: You asking for advice, Chaz?

CHAZ: From *you*? About *ladies*? Yes.

SCOOTS: I mean, just be polite, I guess, and listen to her. And give her gifts sometimes.

CHAZ: Like what?

SCOOTS: Once I got her a crossbow – she really liked that. But I get her smaller stuff too – flowers, chocolates, that kind of thing.

CHAZ: Yeah, that's real good.

SCOOTS: She says she doesn't go in for that stuff, but I can tell she likes it.

CHAZ: So who's your bird?

SCOOTS: Oh, I couldn't say.

CHAZ: So I know her?

SCOOTS: Why would you think that?

CHAZ: Why else can't you tell me? Come on, spill.

SCOOTS: I should study the pitcher.

CHAZ: I'll tell you mine.

SCOOTS: I'm still not saying.

CHAZ: I've been dying to tell someone.

SCOOTS: Yeah?

CHAZ: You'll never guess.

SCOOTS: Then just say.

CHAZ: It's gonna make your nose bleed.

SCOOTS: Just because it bled that once doesn't mean it happens all the time.

CHAZ: If you say so.

SCOOTS: Who is it?

CHAZ: The ump.

SCOOTS: The who?

CHAZ: You know, *the* ump.

SCOOTS: The ump? *The* ump!

CHAZ: Yep.

SCOOTS: Vivien Stahl Von Dieterhoff!

CHAZ: I call her Viv.

SCOOTS: Oh good gosh!

CHAZ: Ain't I somethin'?

SCOOTS: My nose – it's bubbling.

CHAZ: Take it easy.

SCOOTS: The floodgates, they're opening! Oh no!

CHAZ: Just cool it, huh.

SCOOTS: I'm hyperventilating!

CHAZ: Whoa.

SCOOTS: Air! I need air!

CHAZ: Jeez you're a weirdo.

SCOOTS: *(Crumpling to his knees.)* I'm going to faint –

CHAZ: *(Calling off.)* We're gonna need a pinch-hitter here!

    (VIVIEN enters again, agitated.)

VIVIEN: What's wrong with him?

CHAZ: He got dizzy. Must be the pollen.

VIVIEN: He's holding up the game.

CHAZ: I'll help him off.

VIVIEN: Make it snappy.

CHAZ: *(Bending to assist Scoots.)* Oh boy!

VIVIEN: What now?

> *(SCOOTS lifts his head, mopped in blood because of his nose.)*

CHAZ: His face is covered in blood.

VIVIEN: *(Quivering with temptation.)* So I see!

CHAZ: He gets nosebleeds.

VIVIEN: Get him away from me.

CHAZ: It's not serious.

VIVIEN: *(Struggling to restrain herself.)* Get him away from me!

CHAZ: You okay, Viv?

VIVIEN: I'm weak. I'm very weak.

CHAZ: You're out of sorts.

VIVIEN: It's only a spell.

CHAZ: Maybe you should sit down.

VIVIEN: There are things you don't know about me, Chaz.

CHAZ: You look really pale.

VIVIEN: Dreadful, dark things.

CHAZ: More pale than usual even.

VIVIEN: Things you won't understand.

CHAZ: Why are you trembling?

VIVIEN: If they ever come out, know that I'm more than what people will say I am. I have much to give, Chaz. So much.

CHAZ: You're not making sense.

VIVIEN: GET THAT BOY OFF THIS FIELD AND OUT OF MY SIGHT!

(VIVIEN skulks off. CHAZ lifts SCOOTS to his feet and begins to help him off.)

CHAZ: What's with you, nosebleed? You got me in trouble.

SCOOTS: *(Groggy, garbled.)* The scoreboard — must get message to left field scoreboard —

CHAZ: Oh shut up.

SCENE TWELVE

(GRIMM with ABBY at his home. A table has been

set for dinner. ABBY is putting on her witless antics,
wearing a hitting helmet on backward and
chewing her baseball glove.)

GRIMM: Patsy's making his chicken marsala.

ABBY: Chicky chicky.

GRIMM: I can't understand you with that glove in your mouth.

ABBY: Chicky chicky.

GRIMM: Good heavens, Abby.

(PATSY enters, in apron, serving bowls.)

PATSY: Soup's up! It's a yellow squash basil. I think you'll like it.

GRIMM: Patsy, take away Abby's glove.

ABBY: No!

GRIMM: Abby, you know this behavior isn't allowed at the table.

PATSY: I should see to the chicken.

GRIMM: Take away the glove first.

ABBY: Meany!

PATSY: The chicken might –

GRIMM: Patsy.

PATSY: Yes sir. Abby, may I have your glove?

ABBY: Uh-uh!

PATSY: Abby, please.

ABBY: Suck it!

PATSY: I'll have to take it then.

ABBY: Game on!

PATSY: Why don't you just give it –

> *(PATSY reaches for the glove. This turns into a clumsy, prolonged struggle. He eventually takes the glove, after much rankling, and exits with what dignity he can muster. Continuing the charade, ABBY immediately begins to lap up the soup in front of her.)*

GRIMM: I don't know what could be keeping Chaz.

ABBY: Chaz so dumb.

GRIMM: He's our best player.

ABBY: So dumb.

GRIMM: *(Suspicious.)* Why have you come here tonight, Abby? You haven't accepted an invitation to this house in years.

(CHAZ, still in uniform, comes barreling in, ecstatic, holding a piece of paper.)

CHAZ: I'm going to the show!

GRIMM: What's this?

CHAZ: They offered me a contract!

GRIMM: Who did?

CHAZ: The Cleveland Indians! The Majors!

ABBY: Uh-oh.

CHAZ: I'm gonna be a Big Leaguer!

GRIMM: Now hold on there.

CHAZ: No foolin', Chief! This is it!

GRIMM: Sit down, boy, and catch your breath. It's only Cleveland.

CHAZ: No, I gotta phone sis! Can I use your phone, Chief?

GRIMM: You should think this through.

CHAZ: What's to think through? This here – it's a bonafide Big League contract! It's even got the official seal!

GRIMM: Have you signed?

CHAZ: Not yet.

GRIMM: You can't rush these things. Have a seat and I'll read it through with you. *(Handing him a glass.)* Here, have some water.

CHAZ: I thought you'd be happy for me.

GRIMM: I am, my boy, I am! Overjoyed! I just don't want you to get taken by one of these fat cats.

   (PATSY comes rushing in.)

PATSY: Fire! Fire! My chicken marsala's on fire!

GRIMM: Not now, Patsy!

PATSY: The kitchen's in flames!

GRIMM: Well put them out!

PATSY: I can't! It's blazing!

GRIMM: Blazing? How does a chicken become a blaze?

PATSY: Hurry!

GRIMM: *(Throws down his napkin, exiting with Patsy.)* Really, Patsy! Of all the times for this to happen!

PATSY: Don't hate me sir! Please don't hate me!

   (CHAZ, exuberant, gulps the glass of water. He then sits at the table. Sees ABBY staring at him. Nods and

grins as one might at a two year-old. He begins to tap his hand impatiently on the table. ABBY removes her helmet, turns to CHAZ, sternly.)

ABBY: She'll never let you go.

CHAZ: Huh?

ABBY: You heard me.

CHAZ: What're you talking about?

ABBY: What do you think?

CHAZ: Aren't you supposed to be retarded?

ABBY: If she's scorned again she'll wipe us all out, then come for you.

CHAZ: You're messin' with my head.

ABBY: I know about you and your lady blue.

CHAZ: Huh? How?

ABBY: I have someone on the inside.

CHAZ: Nosebleed . . .

ABBY: This puts you in a precarious, yet expedient position.

CHAZ: I don't know any of those words.

ABBY: Chaz, I've never cared for you.

CHAZ: Why ya gotta be saucy?

ABBY: You're a gilded idiot.

CHAZ: Are you being snarky because I knocked you out? That was an accident, you know.

ABBY: Listen to what I'm saying. Inexplicably – and probably calamitously – it's fallen to you to save us.

CHAZ: From who?

ABBY: Your girlfriend.

CHAZ: Viv?

ABBY: Haven't you noticed certain quirks?

CHAZ: About Viv?

ABBY: About Viv.

CHAZ: Well I've never seen her sleep, and she only eats raw meat. And I mean *raw*. Once she got a hold of this possum and didn't even bother to–

ABBY: Lemme show you something. *(ABBY reveals the spot on her neck.)* You see this mark?

CHAZ: Your daddy's got one in the same spot!

ABBY: What's it look like?

CHAZ: A birthmark?

ABBY: Yes, but what's it resemble?

CHAZ: A butterfly eating a salamander.

ABBY: Look closer.

CHAZ: Well, it – it kinda looks like a bite mark.

ABBY: Now we're getting somewhere.

SCENE THIRTEEN

(VIVIEN at home playing Solitaire. She finishes a game, sighs lightly, begins to deal another game. CHAZ stumbles in. It appears he has been drinking and is a bit tipsy.)

VIVIEN: It's late.

CHAZ: Is it?

VIVIEN: It's almost morning.

CHAZ: Then it's almost early.

VIVIEN: You said you'd come straight after dinner.

CHAZ: And here I am.

VIVIEN: The *soiree* lasted all night, did it?

CHAZ: *(Sits and begins taking off his shoes.)* Mr. Grimm was holding court.

VIVIEN: I don't doubt it.

CHAZ: He's got big plans for the Biscuits.

VIVIEN: Yes.

CHAZ: Bold plans.

VIVIEN: Yes.

CHAZ: He's a great man.

VIVIEN: You smell of booze.

CHAZ: If you only knew why.

VIVIEN: Oh?

CHAZ: It was just a sip or two. How was your night?

VIVIEN: You're looking at it.

CHAZ: The picture was good?

VIVIEN: You should go to bed.

CHAZ: I'm wide awake.

VIVIEN: Why are you still in your uniform?

CHAZ: Am I? I didn't even –

VIVIEN: You seem strange.

CHAZ: Forgot to change is all. You know what a lunkhead I am.

VIVIEN: Chaz, is there something you want to tell me?

CHAZ: Uh-uh. Nope. Nothing. Why?

VIVIEN: The sun will be out soon.

CHAZ: Sunrise! That's the name of your stupid movie!

VIVIEN: It's not stupid, Chaz. I don't like it when you drink.

CHAZ: It's called *Sunrise*, but there ain't one in the whole dang thing! So why's it called *Sunrise* when there ain't even a sunrise!

VIVIEN: The sunrise comes at the end.

CHAZ: Sunrises come at the beginning.

VIVIEN: Not this one.

CHAZ: That's stupid.

VIVIEN: Stop using that word for things you don't get.

CHAZ: I can't stay awake through it.

VIVIEN: Your loss.

CHAZ: Wah wah wah.

VIVIEN: After all the man and woman go through, the sun still rises. Its light cuts through the night, promising a second chance. Their union's redeemed. Their love endures. It's artificial, contrived, and sweeps me away each time. I'm a sucker for sap, I guess. *(CHAZ has fallen asleep in the chair; the following is more to herself than to him.)* I've lived long, seen much: wars, storms, plagues and saints. I've watched Rome burn and Bach compose by candlelight. I've known the face of Jack the Ripper and the fragrance of Catherine the Great. I've watched Alexander weep and Josephine Baker dance the Charleston. But I'd give it all up, all the places and all the people, to marvel at one single sunrise. A real one – in color, with UV rays.

(CHAZ begins to snore. VIVIEN rises, retrieves a blanket and covers him. She then adorns a black cloak, checks the room a final time, making certain CHAZ is sleeping, and stealthily exits.)

(A beat passes. CHAZ'S eyes dart open. He quickly puts on his shoes and sets out in secret pursuit.)

SCENE FOURTEEN

(GRIMM with ABBY.)

GRIMM: You think he's up to it?

ABBY: He better be, for our sake.

GRIMM: He seemed awfully frightened, once we convinced him.

ABBY: He's our only chance of finding her tomb.

GRIMM: I don't think he understood your instructions.

ABBY: They were very simple.

GRIMM: He looked confused.

ABBY: He always looks that way. I went through it several times. Play drunk, pass out, and follow her when she goes. Once he locates her coffin, it's easy. All he has to do is –

GRIMM: Stake his lover through the heart.

ABBY: He'll get over it.

GRIMM: How did you know it was her?

ABBY: The signs were there. The first woman umpire pops up in – of all places – Birmingham, Alabama? And just as you'd assembled your best team?

GRIMM: The iron was prime for striking.

ABBY: Plus there was Gash Manley's disappearance. Recall who it was she had an altercation with opening day?

GRIMM: Gash Manley.

ABBY: She did him in – I'd bet my bushels on it.

GRIMM: He's not the only one.

ABBY: There's another?

GRIMM: Burt the Biscuit.

ABBY: He's missing?

GRIMM: We found him in his locker room – dead.

ABBY: Right, because he was harassing her between innings! Never belittle a vampire in public.

GRIMM: Appalling, isn't it?

ABBY: Well, it was a stupid mascot.

GRIMM: How can you say that?

ABBY: I mean, a biscuit? Doesn't exactly fill one with terror.

GRIMM: People loved Burt.

ABBY: Sure they did, but they'd have loved him just as much if he were a tiger or python.

GRIMM: There are no tigers or pythons in Birmingham.

ABBY: What'd you do with him?

GRIMM: Burt? Patsy dumped him in the river.

ABBY: That's a joke, right?

GRIMM: We couldn't have Burt's slaying get out.

ABBY: You're an accessory after the fact!

GRIMM: Hardly.

ABBY: You aided and abetted!

GRIMM: I only covered it up. Besides, who will know? You said yourself – it's only a biscuit.

ABBY: There was a human being inside Burt.

GRIMM: He did have a glow about him, didn't he?

ABBY: You haven't changed a bit.

GRIMM: I wish you wouldn't say that.

ABBY: Listen to us – arguing like we used to.

GRIMM: Making up for lost time.

ABBY: We're beyond hope.

GRIMM: I've missed you.

ABBY: What?

GRIMM: It's true.

ABBY: I wasn't expecting to hear that tonight.

GRIMM: I wish you hadn't felt the need to live this lie.

ABBY: It was either this lie or your lie.

GRIMM: Maybe I've been too harsh with you through the years.

ABBY: And maybe I've been a teeny bit headstrong.

GRIMM: I'll try to do better if you will.

ABBY: I'd like that.

GRIMM: You were mostly always right anyway.

ABBY: I've waited so long for you to say that.

GRIMM: I said mostly, not entirely.

ABBY: But you also said always.

GRIMM: I didn't.

ABBY: You did. You said I was mostly *always* right.

GRIMM: I wouldn't have said that.

ABBY: You just did.

GRIMM: It doesn't make sense.

ABBY: I'm not the one who said it.

GRIMM: You're *usually* right – let's leave it there.

ABBY: Like when I swore a vampire would return to destroy you?

GRIMM: You were very right on that point, I'm afraid.

ABBY: Hard to believe she fell for Chaz.

GRIMM: She has a type.

ABBY: You'd expect a vampire's tastes to be more refined.

GRIMM: Perhaps she's more human than we think. Besides, Chaz isn't so bad. He's handsome, gifted, always inquiring and asking questions.

ABBY: Like "Where do squirrels go at night?"

GRIMM: Something like that. *(He laughs along with his daughter; then, candidly.)* Where *do* squirrels go at night?

ABBY: I'm glad we've had this moment.

GRIMM: Me too.

ABBY: Because if Chaz fails, come tomorrow we're done for.

GRIMM: Speaking of tomorrow, the sun's nearly up. Would you care to see the garden?

ABBY: You kept my garden?

GRIMM: Age dulls a man.

ABBY: Never pegged you for a green thumb.

GRIMM: Bear in mind, it's only spring.

ABBY: I'm impressed. I'd love to see it.

GRIMM: The tulips need another week.

ABBY: You have tulips?

GRIMM: They're my favorite.

ABBY: Mine too. Maybe we should invite Patsy to come along.

GRIMM: He was burned up pretty bad in the fire.

ABBY: Is he alright?

GRIMM: It was just his hands, and his hair, and his eyebrows.

ABBY: Where is he?

GRIMM: In the meat locker, cooling off.

(They begin to head out together.)

ABBY: You should be nicer to him.

GRIMM: He's an imbecile.

ABBY: He's been with you for years.

GRIMM: You just can't help butting in.

ABBY: *(Wryly.)* But you said you missed me . . .

SCENE FIFTEEN

(The opening of this scene is identical to Scene One.

Through a thin, gloomy mist, CHAZ emerges in uniform. Spooked and jittery, he holds his baseball bat cocked and ready to strike as he timidly creeps about searching but wary. As he does, with a thick Southern drawl, he recites the "Lord's Prayer.")

CHAZ: Our Father . . . who art in heaven . . . hallowed be thy name . . . thy Kingdom come . . . thy will be done . . . on earth . . . as it is in heaven . . . Give us this day . . . our daily bread . . . and forgive us our trespasses . . . as we forgive those who trespass against us . . . Lead us not into temptation . . . but deliver us from evil . . . For thine is the Kingdom . . . and the power . . . and the glory . . . for ever and ever . . .

(In an instant, CHAZ is standing before a coffin, nearly bumping into it. Halting, stupefied, he puts his hand to his mouth, muffling a yelp. Collecting himself, he delicately slides the lid open, peers inside – here lies the evil that lurks! Thinking quick, or as quickly as CHAZ is capable, he breaks the bat over his knee, forming a jagged wooden stake. Tossing aside the shards, he raises the stake above his head.)

CHAZ: AMEN!!!

(He brings the stake down, stabbing the body in the coffin. He breathes heavily, adrenaline rushing.)

CHAZ: *(Sotto voce.)* I'll love you always.

(VIVIEN emerges from the back shadows.)

VIVIEN: *(Tersely.)* That's some way of showing it.

CHAZ: Oh God!

VIVIEN: Weren't you expecting me?

CHAZ: Oh God!

VIVIEN: A direct hit.

CHAZ: How did you – I thought you were –

VIVIEN: Right through the heart.

CHAZ: This isn't part of the plan.

VIVIEN: A real Van Helsing.

CHAZ: You saw – ?

VIVIEN: Everything.

CHAZ: But if you're here, who's in there?

VIVIEN: Lift the veil.

CHAZ: Can't you just tell me?

VIVIEN: Lift the veil.

    (Uneasily, he lifts the veil off the corpse in the coffin.)

CHAZ: Oh God! *(On closer inspection.)* I've never seen this person in my life.

VIVIEN: A hobo I feasted on.

CHAZ: You arranged this? You were on to me?

VIVIEN: I suspected.

CHAZ: I didn't want to do this, you have to believe me.

VIVIEN: You went through with it.

CHAZ: The Grimms said I had to.

VIVIEN: I didn't think you'd go through with it.

CHAZ: But, Viv, you're a vampire.

VIVIEN: I'm also a woman. A woman, like any other, who laughs and loves –

CHAZ: – and drinks blood and sleeps in coffins.

VIVIEN: Peccadilloes, I admit.

CHAZ: So now you prey on me, I guess?

VIVIEN: You make it sound tawdry.

CHAZ: Be gentle, huh.

VIVIEN: Oh stop it, Chaz. I'm not going to prey on you. I'm too tired.

CHAZ: So you'll let me go?

VIVIEN: You're here by your own will.

CHAZ: We can be friends.

VIVIEN: Don't say that. It makes you hollow. Friends don't stake each other through the heart! You would have finished me!

CHAZ: They said it was the only way.

VIVIEN: And you believed them.

CHAZ: They said that now that I made the Majors –

VIVIEN: *(Honestly touched.)* You made the Majors . . .

CHAZ: They said you wouldn't let me go. That your wrath would hunt me down. They said –

VIVIEN: They said! They said! What do they know of us? Of the nights we spent? Of the moments we shared? These last weeks – I didn't think I could know such happiness. I came for revenge and instead found –

CHAZ: Humidity?

VIVIEN: Love.

CHAZ: Oh.

VIVIEN: Love, Chaz.

CHAZ: I shouldn't have come here.

VIVIEN: No, I'm glad you did. I'll make it easy for you. *(Removes the stake from the coffin; hands to Chaz.)* Here's your chance. Destroy me! Slay the vampire!

(VIVIEN opens up her arms, with melodramatic flair, offering her bosom for CHAZ to stab.)

CHAZ: You want me to – ?

VIVIEN: It has to be done.

CHAZ: You don't mean it.

VIVIEN: Next week you'll have forgotten all about me. You'll be in the Bigs, living the posh life in –

CHAZ: Cleveland.

VIVIEN: *(Underwhelmed.)* Cleveland? Really? Anyway, I'll be history to you then.

CHAZ: I don't think so.

VIVIEN: I must be erased.

CHAZ: Can't we just part ways?

VIVIEN: Do it, Chaz! Put an end to my anguish! Mortalize me!

CHAZ: *(Reluctantly.)* Okay then.

VIVIEN: You're not really going to do it, are you?

CHAZ: If you really, really want me to.

VIVIEN: Oh, how could you, Chaz?

CHAZ: You said –

VIVIEN: I was being tragically heroic!

CHAZ: I'm so confused. My mind hurts.

VIVIEN: Are you really so hard-hearted?

CHAZ: No – yes – maybe – this is too much! *(Throws the stake down in frustration.)* I figured when I made the majors it'd be the best day of my life. And when I found out, I mean, I was really charged. But something was off, you know, just not right – and I think I know what it was. It was having to leave you.

VIVIEN: Me?

CHAZ: And I couldn't stop thinking of how I was gonna tell you, and how I might, just maybe, possibly, convince you to come with me.

VIVIEN: To Cleveland?

CHAZ: I mean, you're my best coach, my best scout. Without you, I wouldn't be having the year I'm having. Heck, without you, I'd be dead. I owe you a lot.

VIVIEN: *(Meekly.)* Don't be silly –

CHAZ: And you're, well, you're just about the classiest bird I ever known.

VIVIEN: You mean it?

CHAZ: Well, sure I do – but all that was before I knew you were a vampire.

VIVIEN: Does that really change things so much, when you stop and think about it?

CHAZ: I reckon not.

VIVIEN: I'm the same Child of Darkness I've always been.

CHAZ: So you think, maybe, you'd come with me then?

VIVIEN: To Cleveland?

CHAZ: I hear it's a nice place. I'd have to leave tomorrow night.

VIVIEN: I'd like nothing more than to come with you.

CHAZ: You'd have to quit umpiring.

VIVIEN: The game will go on without me. Besides, I'm not accustomed to the Southern heat.

CHAZ: Oh, I just remembered. I got you something.

VIVIEN: For me?

CHAZ: *(Handing over a small box he's pulled from his back pocket.)* On my way to Grimm's. A token of my thanks.

VIVIEN: I never get presents . . .

CHAZ: Go on. Open it.

VIVIEN: Okay then. *(She pulls a small vial from the box.)* It's – oh my.

CHAZ: It's perfume.

VIVIEN: You have no idea how long I've wanted this.

CHAZ: I had to get the smallest bottle, but when we get to Cleveland and I'm making the big dough –

VIVIEN: It's wonderful.

> *(CHAZ takes VIVIEN'S hand, kisses her. She melts into his arms.)*

CHAZ: Maybe some day scientists will invent a potion – you know, like a magic potion – so that a vampire can finally experience a sunrise.

VIVIEN: *(Glowing.)* I think it's already happened.

SCENE SIXTEEN

(DOUG sitting alone in his seat. We hear the organ's "Da-da-da-DA da-DAA!". DOUG, looking on absently, utters no "Charge!")

(A moment passes, and BILL enters. He now appears as an attractive woman, gracefully wearing a modest dress with pearls and earrings. BILL, understandably a bit flushed, makes his way to his seat beside DOUG who, not recognizing BILL, is put out.)

DOUG: Seat's taken.

BILL: Looks empty to me.

DOUG: It's taken.

BILL: *(Sitting.)* Not anymore.

DOUG: Ma'am, that's my – my friend's seat.

BILL: Where's your friend then?

DOUG: He'll be here.

BILL: Well I'll just sit here till he arrives.

DOUG: You don't understand.

BILL: What am I missing?

DOUG: No one but him has sat there in eleven years.

BILL: Doug?

DOUG: How'd you know my name?

BILL: It's me.

DOUG: Huh?

BILL: It's me, Doug.

DOUG: Bill?

BILL: Yep.

DOUG: Bill?

BILL: Yep.

DOUG: You cut-up you! Lookatcha!

BILL: Look at me!

DOUG: You're wearing pearls!

BILL: Am I? I am!

DOUG: Boy you had me wound up good!

BILL: You shoulda seen your face!

DOUG: You should see yours!

BILL: Good to know you kept my seat.

DOUG: I thought you'd be back, once she was gone.

BILL: Who?

DOUG: The she-ump.

BILL: She's gone?

DOUG: It's been a few weeks now.

BILL: Finally got run off, did she?

DOUG: In over her head. Just up and disappeared.

BILL: You don't say.

DOUG: Vanished.

BILL: In like a ghost, out like a ghost.

DOUG: Pretty much sums it up.

BILL: Good riddance.

DOUG: Should've never happened.

BILL: Though she called a very consistent strike zone.

DOUG: That she did, I'll grant her – but still –

BILL: "But still" is right.

DOUG: I mean, come on.

BILL: What else have I missed?

DOUG: Where to start?

BILL: Heard Chaz made the show.

DOUG: He's been lights out in Cleveland.

BILL: I've read about him in the papers.

DOUG: The boy's a hall-of-famer in waiting.

BILL: And we saw him when!

DOUG: We also got us a new General Manager.

BILL: I hadn't heard that. Who is it?

DOUG: A fella named Patsy Beavers. There he is, in the box seats!

> *(PATSY appears, still in his neck brace. Though his hands are bandaged, his eyebrows are missing, and his hair badly misshapen from the fire, he is beaming with pride and joy.)*

PATSY: Hey, whatcha say, Biscuits! Hammina hammina! Let's play like we mean it tonight! Win one for your ole General Manager! Whatcha say! Hammina hammina!

BILL: Why're his eyebrows missing?

DOUG: No one knows.

> *(GRIMM appears next to PATSY, lounging and lazily fanning himself.)*

GRIMM: Patsy, I've a hankering for a fruit cup.

PATSY: I'll get on it, sir, just after the first pitch.

GRIMM: Patsy.

PATSY: Or right away. Will that be green apples or red?

> *(Lights out on GRIMM and PATSY.)*

DOUG: See here, we got us another star in the making.

BILL: Who would that be?

DOUG: Scoots McGhee.

BILL: No way.

DOUG: Kid's on fire.

BILL: Didn't think he had it in him.

DOUG: Fifteen game hitting-streak.

BILL: What's gotten into him?

DOUG: Could be Cupid.

BILL: Ah ha.

DOUG: They say when a ballplayer's in love the bat weighs a feather and the ball's as big as a melon.

(SCOOTS stretching in uniform. ABBY calls to him from the stands.)

ABBY: Hey, McGhee! You too good to give an autograph?

SCOOTS: What're you doing here?

ABBY: Just out for some air.

SCOOTS: I thought you were working on your book tonight.

ABBY: I'll get around to it.

SCOOTS: Why don't you just admit that you like watching me play?

ABBY: The Complete History of Vampires has waited 2,000 years – I think it can wait out a hitting-streak.

SCOOTS: You want that autograph now?

ABBY: After the game maybe?

SCOOTS: You're gonna get yourself a collector's item.

ABBY: I'm betting I get more than that.

SCOOTS: Oh you think, huh?

ABBY: Bring your nose plugs.

    (Lights out on ABBY and SCOOTS.)

DOUG: Bill, um –

BILL: Yeah?

DOUG: I'm not sure how to put this.

BILL: What is it?

DOUG: Your slip is showing.

BILL: *(Adjusting.)* Oh dang, I'm still getting used to this.

DOUG: What exactly *is* this?

BILL: I asked Bea if I could have a few things of her things.

DOUG: Have or borrow?

BILL: Have.

DOUG: And what would be the reason for that?

BILL: It was time for a change.

DOUG: Most people just buy a new car.

BILL: That wouldn't have done it.

DOUG: No?

BILL: For the first time in my life, I feel – *right*.

DOUG: Right.

BILL: I do, Doug. I really do.

DOUG: Well, you're uh – you're uh – you're –

BILL: You don't have to say anything.

DOUG: Pretty. You look real pretty, Bill.

BILL: Thanks.

DOUG: *(Looks away.)* Hasn't been the same without you.

BILL: I had some things to piece together.

DOUG: *(Hurt.)* You went away. You left me.

BILL: I know.

DOUG: You should've let me know why.

BILL: I'm here now.

DOUG: You really should've let me know.

BILL: It's all better now.

DOUG: *(Softly.)* Next time, talk to me, okay Bill?

BILL: Okay Doug.

> *(Pause.)*

DOUG: *(Upbeat.)* Biscuits are playing better ball of late.

BILL: We're finally playing as a unit.

DOUG: Who knows? If we string together a few wins –

BILL: We can get back in the race.

DOUG: It's a long season.

BILL: And anything can happen.

> *(DOUG smiles at BILL. It is a smile that hopes, perhaps even believes, things will be okay. BILL returns this*

smile, before both men redirect their attention to the baseball field.)

(Lights fade to black.)

END OF PLAY

ABOUT THE AUTHOR

Jonathan Yukich's work is published by Smith & Kraus, Playscripts, Inc., Meriwether Press, Eldridge Publishing, Pioneer Drama Service, Indie Theater Now and Batten Publishing. His plays have been produced across the United States and in Canada, Australia, South Africa and Europe. He lives in New Haven, Connecticut where he teaches theatre at the University of New Haven. For more, please visit jonathanyukich.com.

www.ingramcontent.com/pod-product-compliance
Lightning Source LLC
Chambersburg PA
CBHW061736020426
42331CB00006B/1255